COME
THIRSTY

LEADER'S GUIDE

Receive What Your Soul Longs For

COME
THIRSTY

LEADER'S GUIDE

Receive What Your Soul Longs For

Based on the Book by

MAX LUCADO

NELSON REFERENCE & ELECTRONIC
A Division of Thomas Nelson Publishers
Since 1798

www.thomasnelson.com

Published by Thomas Nelson, Inc., P.O. Box 141000, Nashville, Tennessee, 37214.

Library of Congress Cataloging-in-Publication Data is available.

ISBN 1-4185-0029-1

Printed in United States.

1 2 3 4 5 — 08 07 06 05 04

TABLE OF CONTENTS

"Whoever drinks of the water that I shall give him will never thirst. But the water that I shall give him will become in him a fountain of water springing up into everlasting life."

—John 4:14 NKJV

COME THIRSTY READING PLAN

Week 1

♦ Read the Introduction of *Come Thirsty*. As you read through "Meaghan," her story will sound strangely familiar. As this introduction unfolds, we discover a young woman who is thirsting for something real.

♦ Read Chapter 1 of *Come Thirsty*: "The Dehydrated Heart"—Unless we are drinking deeply at the well of God's supply, our hearts become dehydrated—dry, depleted, parched, and weak.

Week 2

♦ Chapter 2: "Sin Vaccination"—We were all born with a terminal disease—hopelessly infected by sin. See how God made a way for us to live disease free.

♦ Chapter 3: "When Grace Goes Deep"—Grace is a gift of God. Take a look at what happens when you try to put conditions on the grace of God. Grace is what defines us.

♦ Chapter 4: "When Death Becomes Birth"—Don't allow the dread of death to take away your joy of living.

♦ Chapter 5: "With Heart Headed Home"—We live caught between what is and what will be. Our hearts are longing for heaven, and every day that passes brings us closer to home.

Week 3

- Chapter 6: "Hope for Tuckered Town"—Some of us try to live our Christian lives completely in our own power. God offers hope for us when the effort wears us down.

- Chapter 7: "Waiting for Power"—Before we move forward, sometimes God asks us to wait … and pray.

- Chapter 8: "God's Body Glove"—The Holy Spirit works with us and through us, hand in glove.

- Chapter 9: "It's Not Up to You"—God paid too high a price for you to leave you unguarded. The Holy Spirit reminds us of our place in God's heart and comes to our aid in times of weakness.

Week 4

- Chapter 10: "In God We (Nearly) Trust"—We know that God knows what's best. We know that we don't. We also know that God cares, so we can trust him.

- Chapter 11: "Worry? You Don't Have To"—Worry changes nothing, and only shows that we aren't trusting God to do as he promised.

- Chapter 12: "Angels Watching Over You"—When you accept God's lordship in your life, you can be assured that many mighty angels will guard you in all your ways.

- Chapter 13: "With God as Your Guardian"—God guards those who turn to him.

Week 5

Prayer of the Thirsty

Lord, I come thirsty. I come to drink, to receive. I receive Your work on the cross and in Your resurrection. My sins are pardoned and my death is defeated. I receive Your energy. Empowered by Your Holy Spirit, I can do all things through Christ who gives me strength. I receive Your lordship. I belong to You. Nothing comes to me that hasn't passed through You. And I receive Your love. Nothing can separate me from Your love. Amen.

INTRODUCTION

Who are we? Busy people. Burdened people. Burned-out people. Strained, stressed, and stretched people, longing for refreshment. These are all symptoms of a dryness deep within. A need. A thirsting. Deprive your soul of spiritual water and it will tell you. Dehydrated hearts send desperate messages. Snarling tempers. Waves of worry. Whispers of guilt and fear. Hopelessness. Sleeplessness. Loneliness. Resentment. Irritability. Insecurity. But God doesn't want us to live like this.

Like the woman at the well, we must recognize our need for living water. Our hearts are parched, dry, dehydrated. We need moisture, a swallow of water, a long, quenching drink. And where do we find water for the soul? "If anyone thirsts, let him come to Me and drink. He who believes in Me, as the Scripture has said, out of his heart will flow rivers of living water" (John 7:37, 38 NKJV). Jesus invites: *Are your insides starting to shrivel?* Drink me. What H_2O can do for your body, Jesus can do for your heart. Come and see what the Lord can do in your heart! Come ready to receive the refreshment your soul longs for. Come, and come thirsty.

W-E-L-L

Receive Christ's Work on the cross.

Receive the Energy of his Spirit.

Receive his Lordship over your life.

Receive his unending, unfailing Love.

Week 1

Thirsting After Righteousness

*"Blessed are those who hunger
and thirst for righteousness,
for they shall be filled."*

—Matthew 5:6 NKJV

Introduction

Have you ever been in the mood for ... *something* ... to eat? You've got the munchies, and you're looking for a snack. The only problem is that you're not quite sure what will satisfy your craving. Something salty? Something sweet? Something chewy? Something crunchy? It's hard to put your finger on what's driving you to rummage through the pantry. Nothing looks good, so you slam through the cupboards and poke around in the back of the fridge.

Our souls are not so different. We get a restless yearning for ... *something*. Our hearts are hungry. We are driven by a deep thirst. And so we cast about for

Opening Class

Option 1

Have you ever been hungry for something, but had a hard time putting your finger on just what it was? What kinds of quirky food cravings have you had?

Option 2

Read the story of the woman at the well (John 4:4–26), and compare it together to the story of Meaghan, from the introduction to *Come Thirsty*.

Option 3

There is something powerful about reading Scripture out loud together. Have people in the group look up this week's Scripture passages in various translations. Use them as a starting point for your lesson.

"You gave them bread from heaven for their hunger, and brought them water out of the rock for their thirst."

—Nehemiah 9:15 NKJV

something to satisfy our need. If we do not nourish our soul, it grows weak and weary. Deprived of sustenance, we become strained, stretched, and stressed. Scripture compares this desperate need with thirst. Are you thirsty?

1. Remember the children of Israel, wandering in the wilderness for forty years. They understood what it meant to be hungry and thirsty. "Hungry and thirsty, their soul fainted in them" (Ps. 107:5 NKJV). How does Isaiah 29:8 describe the hunger and thirst of men?

   "When a ____hungry____ man dreams, and look—he ____eats____; but he ____eats____, and his soul is still ____empty____; or as when a ____thirsty____ man dreams, and look—he ____drinks____; but he ____awakes____, and indeed he is ____faint____, and his soul still ____craves____." (NKJV)

2. Yet God provided for the physical needs of those who called upon him for relief. The people's dehydrated bodies longed for water, and that is just what God supplied. Match up these promises for refreshment with their texts.

2

_d_ Nehemiah 9:15   a. God didn't withhold the water from the thirsty.

_a_ Nehemiah 9:20   b. When God led in deserts, they didn't go thirsty.

_f_ Isaiah 41:17   c. Everyone who thirsts, come to the waters.

_b_ Isaiah 48:21   d. You brought them water out of the rock.

_e_ Isaiah 49:10   e. God has mercy, and leads by springs of water.

_c_ Isaiah 55:1   f. The needy seek water; their tongues fail for thirst.

Reading Scripture Out Loud Together

- **John 4:13, 14**: "Jesus answered, 'Everyone who drinks this water will be thirsty again, but whoever drinks the water I give will never be thirsty. The water I give will become a spring of water gushing up inside that person, giving eternal life'" (NCV).

God supplies our physical needs, sometimes in miraculous ways. Yet there are times when that doesn't feel like enough. "You have planted much, but you harvest little. You eat, but you do not become full. You drink, but you are still thirsty. You put on clothes, but you are not warm enough. You earn money, but then you lose it all as if you had put it into a purse full of holes" (Hag. 1:6 NCV). We have food to eat and water to drink, but they do not satisfy the longing that pervades our soul. We are thirsty, but for what? Where should we turn for relief?

"Deprive your body of necessary fluid, and your body will tell you. Deprive your soul of spiritual water and your soul will tell you."

• **John 7:37, 38**: "On the last and most important day of the feast Jesus stood up and said in a loud voice, 'Let anyone who is thirsty come to me and drink. If anyone believes in me, rivers of living water will flow out from that person's heart, as the Scripture says'" (NCV).

"Blessed are those who hunger and thirst for righteousness, for they shall be filled."

—Matthew 5:6 NKJV

3. Unfortunately, too many try to quench that restless hunger and nagging thirst with things that cannot satisfy. What does Paul say will be the end of those who pursue their appetites for earthly things, according to Philippians 3:19? <u>If we don't grasp the spiritual nature of our longing, we can too easily be lured aside by earthly things which cannot satisfy our thirst. "Whose end is destruction, whose god is their belly, and whose glory is in their shame—who set their mind on earthly things" (Phil. 3:19 NKJV).</u>

Jesus told his followers, "Blessed are you who hunger now, for you shall be filled" (Luke 6:21 NKJV). What a wonderful promise! But moments later, he turned this statement upside down. "Woe to you who are full, for you shall hunger" (Luke 6:25 NKJV). Consider this. Those who are satisfied with what the world has to offer, no longer hunger and thirst after spiritual things. They opted for a shortcut. They settled for instant gratification. Those of us who continue to thirst after the living water only Jesus can supply will rely upon him right on into eternity. Our hunger will be satisfied in the very presence of God.

4. David understood the longing of his heart. He knew exactly what he was thirsty for.

♦ According to Psalm 42:2, what did David thirst for?

"I thirst for the living God. When can I go to meet with him?" (Ps. 42:2 NCV).

♦ To what did David compare his longing in Psalm 143:6?

David thirsted for God. "I lift my hands to you in prayer. As a dry land needs rain, I thirst for you" (Ps. 143:6 NCV).

♦ What did David do, in an effort to assuage his longing for God, according to Psalm 63:1?

David compares his longing for God to that of drought-stricken lands, eager and desperate for the rains. "God, you are my God. I search for you. I thirst for you like someone in a dry, empty land where there is no water" (Ps. 63:1 NCV).

- **Matthew 5:6**: "Blessed are those who hunger and thirst for righteousness, For they shall be filled" (NKJV).

- **Matthew 6:33**: "But seek first the kingdom of God and His righteousness, and all these things shall be added to you" (NKJV).

- **Titus 3:5**: "Not by works of righteousness which we have done, but according to His mercy He saved us" (NKJV).

5. So what should we be hungering for? What should we be thirsting after? Jesus tells us in Matthew 5:6.

"Blessed are those who hunger and thirst for righteousness, for they shall be filled" (Matt. 5:6 NKJV).

There's no denying the urgency of our thirst. We should heed it. We should drink. But when seeking to quench our thirsty hearts, we must be certain to drink good water. There can be no substitutes. If you are

Discussion Questions

- When can you tell that your heart is becoming dehydrated? What are the symptoms of spiritual thirst in your own life?

- Make sure that everyone in your group understands the theme of the *Come Thirsty* Curriculum. Give them the overview:

"He shall bring forth your righteousness as the light, and your justice as the noonday."

—Psalm 37:6 NKJV

indeed thirsting after righteousness, then the Lord urges you to drink, and drink deeply.

6. Jesus tells us, "Seek first the kingdom of God and His righteousness" (Matt. 6:33 NKJV). So, what is righteousness? Match up these passages, which give us a little overview.

  c   Psalm 11:7   a. The heavens declare His righteousness.

  f   Proverbs 11:19   b. The sun of righteousness shall rise.

  h   Psalm 48:10   c. The LORD is righteous. He loves righteousness.

  a   Psalm 50:6   d. God has given us a robe of righteousness.

  e   Psalm 65:5   e. God works awesome deeds in righteousness.

  i   Psalm 119:172   f. Righteousness leads to life.

  d   Isaiah 61:10   g. He will be called: the LORD Our Righteousness.

  g   Jeremiah 23:6   h. God's right hand is full of righteousness.

  b   Malachi 4:2   i. All of God's commandments are righteousness.

Our first tendency in seeking righteousness is to try to *do* something. But the Lord is not asking us to do anything. We are called upon to receive what he has provided. "Not by works of righteousness which we have done, but according to his mercy he saved us" (Titus 3:5 NKJV).

7. We need to cultivate a hunger and a thirst for righteousness, but we cannot achieve a righteous and godly life without divine assistance.

    ♦ What does God give to us, according to Psalm 24:5?
    <u>"He shall receive blessing from the LORD, and righteousness from the God of his salvation" (Ps. 24:5 NKJV).</u>

    ♦ God doesn't leave us to fend for ourselves. What does Psalm 23:3 say He will do for us?
    <u>"He restores my soul; He leads me in the paths of righteousness for His name's sake" (Ps. 23:3 NKJV).</u>

    ♦ What glorious promise do we find in Psalm 37:6?
    <u>"He shall bring forth your righteousness as the light, and your justice as the noonday" (Ps. 37:6 NKJV).</u>

Throughout the course of this study, we will be seeking out four ways in which our thirst can be satisfied. God's work. God's energy. His lordship and his love. You'll find them easy to remember. Just think of the word W-E-L-L.

*Receive Christ's **W**ork on the cross.*

*The **E**nergy of his Spirit.*

*His **L**ordship over your life.*

*His unending, unfailing **L**ove.*

Drink deeply and often. And out of you will flow rivers of living water.

"Now I am right with God, not because I followed the law, but because I believed in Christ. God uses my faith to make me right with him."

—Philippians 3:9 NCV

7

- We have been raised with adages like "If it sounds too good to be true, it probably is" and "there's no such thing as a free lunch." Do you think this affects our understanding of grace? Do you feel as if you should have to do something to earn your way into God's favor?

- Saturating yourself in worldly things dulls your appetite for the good and the righteous. Have you ever tried to satisfy your spiritual longing with other things? What kinds of substitutes have you busied yourself with?

"In order for Jesus to do what water does, you must let him go where water goes. Deep, deep inside."

8. Throughout the New Testament, we are told that righteousness and right living are only possible by the grace of God. All we need to do is believe. Paul assures us that it is by faith that we are made righteous.

Romans 10:10: "We ___believe___ with our ___hearts___; and so we are ___made right___ with God. And we use our mouths to say that we ___believe___, and so we are ___saved___" (Rom. 10:10 NCV).

2 Corinthians 5:21: "He made Him who ___knew___ no ___sin___ to be ___sin___ for us, that we might ___become___ the ___righteousness___ of God in Him" (2 Cor. 5:21 NKJV).

Ephesians 4:23, 24: You were taught to be ___made new___ in your ___hearts___; to become a ___new person___. That ___new person___ is made to be ___like God___—made to be truly <u>good</u> and <u>holy</u>" (Eph. 4:23, 24 NCV).

Philippians 3:9: "Not having my own ___righteousness___, which is from the law, but that which is through ___faith___ in ___Christ___, the ___righteousness___ which is from ___God___ by ___faith___" (Phil. 3:9 NKJV)

There is some danger that a gift so freely given can be taken too much for granted. We can become numb to our thirst for a time. We can sink into apathy and lethargy. Scripture uses hunger and thirst to convey a sense of urgency. We are dependent upon God. We cannot live without him. We need him. In order to keep those truths before us, we must cultivate our appetite for righteousness. Stir up your hunger. Heed your thirst. Drink, and keep on drinking!

9. Do we hunger and thirst after righteousness? Yes! So what *can* we do about it? Pursue it!

   ♦ What does Paul urge his son in the faith to pursue in 1 Timothy 6:11?
   <u>"Flee these things and pursue righteousness, godliness, faith, love, patience, gentleness" (1 Tim. 6:11 NKJV).</u>

   ♦ What did Jesus do in order to make our pursuit possible, according to 1 Peter 2:24?
   <u>Set aside earthly distractions and satisfy your thirst with good things. "Who Himself bore our sins in His own body on the tree, that we, having died to sins, might live for righteousness" (1 Pet. 2:24 NKJV).</u>

   ♦ Where can we turn for help in our pursuit, according to 2 Timothy 3:16?

• Our hearts are hungry and thirsty—that's undeniable. But how do we cultivate a hunger and thirst for the right things—for righteousness?

Open It Up to Questions

Does anyone have any questions that came up over the week while reading either the book or the daily devotional readings?

<u>We could not live for righteousness if Jesus hadn't borne our sins on the cross. "All Scripture is given by inspiration of God, and is profitable for doctrine, for reproof, for correction, for instruction in righteousness" (2 Tim. 3:16 NKJV). God did not leave us wandering and wondering what to do. Everything we need to know for righteous living can be found throughout the pages of his Word.</u>

10. Jesus is the source of everything we need. He calls to everyone, urging them to come.

    ♦ What did Jesus call out to the people in John 7:37?

    <u>"Jesus stood and cried out, saying, 'If anyone thirsts, let him come to Me and drink'"</u>

    <u>(John 7:37 NKJV).</u>

    ♦ According to Revelation 21:6, what does Jesus say that He will freely give?

    <u>"I will give of the fountain of the water of life freely to him who thirsts" (Rev. 21:6 NKJV).</u>

    ♦ Who is invited to come and drink, according to Revelation 22:17?

    <u>"The Spirit and the bride say, 'Come!' And let him who hears say, 'Come!' And let him who thirsts come. Whoever desires, let him take the water of life freely" (Rev. 22:17 NKJV).</u>

Conclusion

Do you remember the woman at the well? Jesus made an outlandish claim to her: "Whoever drinks of this water will thirst again, but whoever drinks of the water that I shall give him will never thirst. But the water that I shall give him will become in him a fountain of water springing up into everlasting life" (John 4:13, 14 NKJV). Like the woman at the well, we recognize our need for living water. We need moisture, a swallow of water, a long, quenching drink. But where do we find water for the soul?

Throughout the course of this study, we will be seeking out four ways in which our thirst can be satisfied. God's work. God's energy. His lordship and his love. You'll find them easy to remember. Just think of the word W-E-L-L.

Receive Christ's **W**ork on the cross.
The **E**nergy of his Spirit.
His **L**ordship over your life.
His unending, unfailing **L**ove.

Drink deeply and often. And out of you will flow rivers of living water.

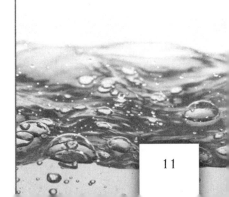

Prayer of the Thirsty

This is the prayer of the thirsty soul who has turned to the only Source of living water. It is the prayer of a heart ready to receive—to drink deeply from the well of God's work, energy, lordship, and love. Take the time each day to pray this prayer aloud. Learn what a vast resource God has made available to you. Make it the cry of your heart.

Lord, I come thirsty. I come to drink, to receive. I receive Your work on the cross and in Your resurrection. My sins are pardoned and my death is defeated. I receive Your energy. Empowered by Your Holy Spirit, I can do all things through Christ who gives me strength. I receive Your lordship. I belong to You. Nothing comes to me that hasn't passed through You. And I receive Your love. Nothing can separate me from Your love.

This Week's Prayer Requests

Memory Verse

"Jesus stood and cried out, saying, 'If anyone thirsts, let him come to Me and drink. He who believes in Me, as the Scripture has said, out of his heart will flow rivers of living water.'"

— John 7:37, 38 NKJV

Suggested Reading for this Week from *Come Thirsty* by Max Lucado:

- Read the Introduction of *Come Thirsty*: "Meaghan"—As you read through "Meaghan," her story will sound strangely familiar. As this introduction unfolds, we discover a young woman who is thirsting for something real.

- Read Chapter 1 of *Come Thirsty*: "The Dehydrated Heart"—Unless we are drinking deeply at the well of God's supply, our hearts become dehydrated—dry, depleted, parched, and weak.

W-E-L-L

Receive Christ's Work on the cross.

WEEK 2

GRACE BLOCKERS

*"For by grace you have been
saved through faith, and that not
of yourselves; it is the gift of God."*

—Ephesians 2:8 NKJV

Introduction

Your heart is thirsty, so you make your way to
the water fountain of God's grace for a drink. You've
been there before. It's an abundant source of living
water. Crystal clear streams forever flowing into shining
pools at the foot of the throne. Drinking deeply of
God's grace is just what your soul needs right now.
The recollection of its plentiful supply and satisfying
coolness quickens your step. But as you draw near,
you're astonished to find a handmade sign taped
crookedly to the fountain's edge. "No swallowing,
please. Taste, but don't drink." You look around,
wondering if this can be a prank—someone's idea of
a joke. Shrugging, you dip into the cooling water, but

Option 1
  Rules, rules, rules! Have
  you ever run up against
  a rule or law that you
  thought was a little
  absurd? Share some
  with the group.

Option 2
  Have you ever looked at
  the plan of salvation and
  thought, "Is that all there
  is to it?" "Why isn't something with eternal reper-
  cussions more compli-
  cated?" How is the gift
  of God's grace simple?

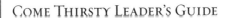

Option 3

There is something powerful about reading Scripture out loud together. Have people in the group look up this week's Scripture passages in various translations. Use them as a starting point for your lesson.

only enough to wet your lips. And so you turn back, your disappointed heart still longing for refreshment.

Does such a sign sound absurd? It should. But that's what happens when people try to place limitations on God's grace. They block up the fountain of grace. They monitor our every sip. They stand by with arms folded, directing us to swish and spit, when all the while God intended us to drink, and drink deeply.

1. Let's start with grace—unmerited favor. What does the New Testament teach us about the grace of God that is extended toward us? Match up these truths with the verse in which it can be found.

<u>k</u> 1 Corinthians 15:10   a. Because of grace, we have everlasting hope.

<u>e</u> Ephesians 1:6   b. By grace we have been made heirs.

<u>c</u> Colossians 3:16   c. Sing to the Lord with grace in your hearts.

<u>h</u> Colossians 4:6   d. Grace was ours even before time began.

<u>a</u> 2 Thessalonians 2:16   e. By grace, we are accepted in the Beloved.

_d_ 2 Timothy 1:9

_j_ 2 Timothy 2:1

_b_ Titus 3:7

_g_ Hebrews 4:16

_i_ 1 Peter 1:13

_f_ 1 Peter 4:10

f. Be good stewards of God's manifold grace.

g. We can approach the throne of grace boldly.

h. Let your speech always be with grace.

i. Rest your hope fully upon grace.

j. Be strong in grace.

k. By the grace of God, I am what I am.

2. What good is grace if you don't let it go deep? Look at these verses, and more specifically, look at the words used to describe God's grace.

Romans 3:24: "Being justified <u>freely</u> by His grace" (Rom. 3:24 NKJV).

Romans 5:20: "Where sin abounded, grace <u>abounded</u> <u>much more</u>" (Rom. 5:20 NKJV).

Reading Scripture Out Loud

• **1 Peter 1:13**: "So prepare your minds for service and have self-control. All your hope should be for the gift of grace that will be yours when Jesus Christ is shown to you" (NCV).

• **2 Corinthians 9:8**: "God is able to make all grace abound toward you, that you, always having all sufficiency in all things, may have an abundance for every good work" (NKJV).

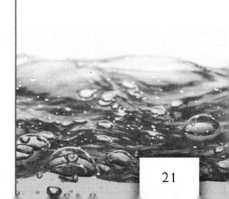

21

- **Romans 11:6**: "If by grace, then it is no longer of works; otherwise grace is no longer grace. But if it is of works, it is no longer grace; otherwise work is no longer work" (NKJV).

- **Ephesians 2:7**: "That in the ages to come He might show the exceeding riches of His grace in His kindness toward us in Christ Jesus" (NKJV).

- **1 Timothy 1:14**: "The grace of our Lord was exceedingly abundant" (NKJV).

2 Corinthians 9:8: "God is able to make all __grace__ __abound__ toward you, that you, always having __all sufficiency__ in __all__ things, may have an __abundance__ for __every__ good work" (2 Cor. 9:8 NKJV).

Ephesians 2:7: "That in the ages to come He might show the __exceeding__ riches of His grace in His kindness toward us in Christ Jesus" (Eph. 2:7 NKJV).

1 Timothy 1:14: "The grace of our Lord was __exceedingly abundant__" (1 Tim. 1:14 NKJV).

Abundant. Free. Sufficient. Rich. God's grace is excessive—more plentiful than our need. In fact, it is all we need. But there were those in the early church who tried to staunch the flow of grace. They wanted to impose limits. They tried to control it. They molded it to fit into their traditions. They redefined it to suit their purposes. And they deceived God's people by touting it as truth.

3. What new rules did some try to impose on Gentile believers, according to Acts 15:1? **"Then some people came to Antioch from Judea and began teaching the non-Jewish believers: 'You cannot be saved if you are not circumcised as Moses taught us'" (Acts 15:1 NCV). How outrageous! There is no commandment of God that says, "Thou shalt be circumcised, or thou canst become a Christian." They tried to adapt grace to fit into their traditions, and received an apostolic rebuke for it.**

4. The Galatian church also ran into problems. Paul was astonished by how far off track they had been lured.

   Galatians 1:6, 7: "God, by his grace through Christ, called you to become his people. So I am __amazed__ that you are __turning away__ so quickly and believing something __different__ than the __Good News__. Really, there is __no other__ Good News. But some people are __confusing__ you; they want to __change__ the Good News of Christ" (Gal. 1:6, 7 NCV).

Discussion Questions

- There are those who block grace by putting limitations and requirements on it. Sometimes this is referred to as legalism. How would you define legalism?

- In the New Testament, the Pharisees are the epitome of legalism. How did their adamant adherence to rules, regulations, and traditions cause trouble between them and Jesus?

- What is the difference between Christ's work *for* you and Christ's work *in* you?

- There are voices that condemn us. There are voices that make us feel guilty. There are voices that accuse us. There are voices that mock us. What do those voices say to you?

- Is there a difference between what those voices tell us about ourselves and what God says about us? Who does God say that you are?

Legalism. Grace blockage. It's thinking that your Heavenly Father might let you in the gate, but you've got to earn your place at the table. God makes the down payment on your redemption, but you still have to pay the monthly installments. Heaven gives the boat, but you've got to row it if you ever want to see the other shore. They don't allow you to receive God's work. They try to tell you to earn it.

5. Grace, by definition, excludes our efforts to earn it. Why does Paul say that grace cannot come by works in Romans 11:6?
   "If by grace, then it is no longer of works; otherwise grace is no longer grace. But if it is of works, it is no longer grace; otherwise work is no longer work" (Rom. 11:6 NKJV). If grace had to be earned, it couldn't be called grace. As another translation puts it, "If they could be made God's people by what they did, God's gift of grace would not really be a gift" (NCV).

Grace by faith is one of Paul's most adamant themes. "People cannot do any work that will make them right with God. So they must trust in him, who makes even evil people right in his sight. Then God accepts their faith, and that makes them right with him" (Rom. 4:5 NCV). One way, and only one. By grace, through faith.

6. Why does Ephesians 2:8, 9 say we have no reason to boast over our place in God's family?

<u>"For by grace you have been saved through faith, and that not of yourselves; it is the gift of God, not of works, lest anyone should boast" (Eph. 2:8, 9 NKJV). How can you boast about something you did not do? God did all the work. All we did was receive the gift.</u>

Beware when faith changes from grace receiving to law keeping. Take care when salvation is limited to those who can meet the standards and accomplish the tasks. We cannot earn God's grace. We can only receive God's work. That's when our hearts are able to drink deeply from the well of living water.

7. What is the work that we must receive? Christ's work on the cross. Or to ask the question as we find it in Scripture, "What must I do to be saved?" (Acts 16:30 NKJV).

♦ How is this question answered in Acts 16:31?
<u>"Believe in the Lord Jesus and you will be saved" (Acts 16:31 NCV).</u>

♦ According to 2 Corinthians 5:21, how were we freed from sin?
<u>"Christ had no sin, but God made him become sin so that in Christ we could become right with God" (2 Cor. 5:21 NCV).</u>

Open It Up to Questions

Does anyone have any questions that came up over the week while reading either the book or the daily devotional readings?

♦ What did Jesus say we must believe in order to be saved, according to John 8:24?
<u>"I told you that you would die in your sins. Yes, you will die in your sins if you don't believe that I am he" (John 8:24 NCV). Salvation hinges on Jesus Christ and our belief. Do you believe he is who he said he is? Have you received God's grace by faith?</u>

And so our sins are forgiven. Christ responded to universal sin with a universal sacrifice, taking on the sins of the entire world. This is Christ's work *for* you. But the salvation we receive doesn't stop there. Jesus not only took your place on the cross, he takes his place in your heart. This is Christ's work *in* you.

8. How does Paul describe those who have drunk deeply at the well of grace?

♦ What does Romans 4:7 say about those who have received Christ's work *for* us?
<u>"Happy are they whose sins are forgiven, whose wrongs are pardoned" (Rom. 4:7 NCV).</u>

"God refuses to compromise the spiritual purity of heaven. Herein lies the awful fruit of sin. Lead a godless life and expect a godless eternity. Spend a life telling God to leave you alone and He will."

⬦ How has our life been changed by Christ's work *in* us, according to Romans 6:6?

 <u>The New King James Version reads, "Blessed are those whose lawless deeds are forgiven, and whose sins are covered" (Rom. 4:7 NKJV). That is Christ's work for us. And what of His work in us? "We know that our old life died with Christ on the cross so that our sinful selves would have no power over us and we would not be slaves to sin" (Rom. 6:6 NCV).</u>

You will occasionally sin. And when you do, remember: sin may touch, but cannot claim you. Christ is in you! Trust his work *for* you. He took your place on the cross. And trust his work *in* you. Your heart is his home, and his home is sin free.

9. There are many voices telling you who you should be and what you should do. Which ones have you heard lately? Which ones have you been listening to?

   ❏ You don't do enough.
   ❏ You don't fit in.
   ❏ You don't meet the standard.
   ❏ You ought to know better.
   ❏ You've made too many mistakes.
   ❏ You've got to try harder.
   ❏ You're not doing it the right way.
   ❏ You're not making a difference.

"Sin may, and will, touch you, discourage you, distract you, but it cannot condemn you."

27

- ❏ You're not smart enough.
- ❏ You need to snap out of it.
- ❏ What would people think?
- ❏ What were you thinking?
- ❏ It's your own fault.
- ❏ It's too late.
- ❏ I told you so.

<u>Other people are very willing to let you know what they think of you and of your choices. They point out your flaws. They dig up past mistakes. They tell you what they would do in your place. But they cannot define you. Grace defines you. Only God can tell you who you are. His is the only opinion that matters.</u>

You are who *God* says you are. Grace defines you. People may have opinions, but they hold no clout. Only God does. His is the only opinion that matters, and according to him, you are his. Period.

10. Who does God say you are? What does Ephesians 2:10 say?

    <u>"God has made us what we are. In Christ Jesus, God made us to do good works, which God planned in advance for us to live our lives doing" (Eph. 2:10 NCV). We are who God made us to be. Unique. Special. Gifted for a purpose. Planned on. In other translations, we are God's "workmanship," his "handiwork," his "masterpiece."</u>

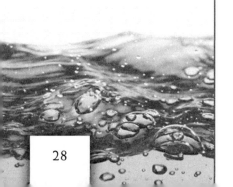

Conclusion

Receive God's work. Drink deeply from his well of grace. Your deeds don't save you. And your deeds don't keep you saved. God does. Can I urge you to trust this truth? Let your constant prayer be this: "Lord, I receive Your work. My sins are pardoned." Trust the work of God for you. Then trust the presence of Christ in you. Take frequent, refreshing drinks from his well of grace. You need regular reminders that you are not fatally afflicted! Don't live like you are.

Prayer of the Thirsty

Return to this prayer, paying close attention to the heartfelt meaning in the first few sentences. You came to God thirsty, and he answers you with the satisfying work of grace. Savor Christ's work for you and in you. Let the truth of salvation refresh your soul.

> *Lord, I come thirsty. I come to drink, to receive. I receive Your work on the cross and in Your resurrection. My sins are pardoned and my death is defeated. I receive Your energy. Empowered by Your Holy Spirit, I can do all things through Christ who gives me strength. I receive Your lordship. I belong to You. Nothing comes to me that hasn't passed through You. And I receive Your love. Nothing can separate me from Your love.*

THIS WEEK'S PRAYER REQUESTS

Memory Verse

*"For by grace you have been saved
through faith, and that not of
yourselves; it is the gift of God, not
of works, lest anyone should boast.
For we are His workmanship, created
in Christ Jesus for good works,
which God prepared beforehand
that we should walk in them."*

—Ephesians 2:8–10 NKJV

Suggested Reading for this Week from *Come Thirsty* by Max Lucado:

- Chapter 2: "Sin Vaccination"—We were all born with a terminal disease—hopelessly infected by sin. See how God made a way for us to live disease free.
- Chapter 3: "When Grace Goes Deep"— Grace is a gift of God. Take a look at what happens when you try to put conditions on the grace of God. Grace is what defines us.
- Chapter 4: "When Death Becomes Birth"— Don't allow the dread of death to take away your joy of living.
- Chapter 5: "With Heart Headed Home"—We live, caught between what is and what will be. Our hearts are longing for heaven, and every day that passes brings us closer to home.

W-E-L-L

Receive the Energy of his Spirit.

Week 3

Redefining Prayer

"'Not by might nor by
power, but by My Spirit,'
says the LORD of hosts."

—Zechariah 4:6 NKJV

Introduction

We don't like living tired. We were made to flourish and thrive. But when we do not draw from the well of God's provision, spiritual thirst leaves us drained, dry, and drawn. Wobbly-kneed weakness replaces our vitality. Lackluster living steals away our vibrancy. In our feebleness, we can be bowled over by the slightest of disturbances. We cling to wispy willpower, only to be blown off course by a breeze. We don't like living tired, but we do. Why? Because we do not ask for the energy we need. God's energy. Pulsing power. Supernatural strength. And how do we ask the Father for this supply? We pray.

1. Jesus promised his disciples that he would provide them with the power they needed.

Opening Class

Option 1
Slang often takes a common, everyday word and redefines it? What are some of the sillier slang words you can recall, and how did their meanings change?

Option 2
Waiting can be hard, but waiting can also be worthwhile. What things do you consider worth waiting for?

Option 3

There is something powerful when reading Scripture out loud together. Have people in the group look up this week's Scripture passages in various translations. Use them as a starting point for your lesson.

Luke 24:49: "Behold I send the __Promise__ of My Father upon you; but tarry in the city of Jerusalem until you are __endued__ with __power__ from __on high__ " (Luke 24:49 NKJV).

Acts 1:8: ""You shall __receive power__ when the __Holy Spirit__ has __come upon__ you" (Acts 1:8 NKJV).

When does power come? Thankfully, it's not up to us to generate this energetic life. It is a gift from God, and we need only receive it. Power comes as we allow the God who saved us to change us. Power comes as we allow his Spirit to work in us. Power comes when we get rid of harbored sin through confession. Power comes when we unceasingly seek God's Spirit. And power comes when we pray.

"Pray in the Spirit at all times with all kinds of prayers, asking for everything you need. To do this you must always be ready and never give up.

—Ephesians 6:18 NCV

2. Power comes as you pray. What does Paul urge every believer to do in these verses?

- ◆ Romans 12:12: <u>Pray! "Pray at all times"</u> <u>(Rom. 12:12 NCV).</u>

- ◆ Ephesians 6:18: <u>"Pray in the Spirit at all</u> <u>times with all kinds of prayers, asking for</u> <u>everything you need. To do this you must</u> <u>always be ready and never give up (Eph.</u> <u>6:18 NCV).</u>

- ◆ 1 Thessalonians 5:17: <u>"Pray continually"</u> <u>(1 Thess. 5:17 NCV).</u>

3. David pleads with God to hear him: "Hear me when I call, O God of my righteousness! ... Have mercy on me, and hear my prayer" (Ps. 4:1 NKJV). We need to pray continually and with confidence.

Reading Scripture Out Loud

- **Ephesians 6:18**: "Pray in the Spirit at all times with all kinds of prayers, asking for everything you need. To do this you must always be ready and never give up" (NCV).

- **Jeremiah 29:12**: "You will call upon Me, and go and pray to Me, and I will listen to you" (NKJV).

"God never promises an absence of distress. But he does promise the assuring presence of his Holy Spirit."

• **Romans 8:26**: "The Spirit also helps in our weaknesses. For we do not know what we should pray for as we ought, but the Spirit Himself makes intercession for us with groanings which cannot be uttered" (NKJV).

• **Psalm 27:8**: "When You said, 'Seek My face,' My heart said to You, 'Your face, LORD, I will seek'" (NKJV).

"The Spirit helps us with our weakness. We do not know how to pray as we should. But the Spirit himself speaks to God for us, even begs God for us with deep feelings that words cannot explain."

—Romans 8:26 NCV

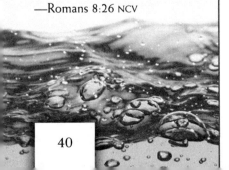

♦ According to Jeremiah 29:12, what does God do?
"You will call upon Me, and go and pray to Me, and I will listen to you" (Jer. 29:12 NKJV).

♦ God hears our prayers, but he also responds. When does Isaiah 65:24 say God answered the call of his people?
"It shall come to pass that before they call, I will answer; and while they are still speaking, I will hear" (Is. 65:24 NKJV).

♦ Because of Jesus' sacrifice, we can approach God with confidence. How does Hebrews 4:16 tell us to go about finding the help we need?
"Let us therefore come boldly to the throne of grace, that we may obtain mercy and find grace to help in time of need" (Heb. 4:16 NKJV)

None of us prays as much as we should, but all of us pray more than we think. In those times when we gasp and sigh and moan. When tears slide silently down our cheeks. When our whole heart aches with need. When the urgency of our situation defies words. Those are the times when the Spirit comes alongside and helps us in our weakness.

4. Just how does the Spirit help us, according to Romans 8:26?

<u>"The Spirit also helps in our weaknesses. For we do not know what we should pray for as we ought, but the Spirit Himself makes intercession for us with groanings which cannot be uttered" (Rom. 8:26 NKJV). The Spirit prays with us and for us. He makes sure we get heard.</u>

Prayer is commonly earmarked as a spiritual discipline. We admire those saints who dedicate hours to intercession, and we feel guilty because we do not. We all want to spend more time in prayer. But who has time to sit serenely, hands clasped and eyes shut? Do this. Change your definition of prayer. Think of prayers as less an activity *for* God and more an awareness *of* God. Seek to live in uninterrupted awareness. Acknowledge his presence everywhere you go.

5. God promised to be present with those who belong to him. Yet some people dash headlong through life, never seeing or acknowledging God's hand. But those who are aware of God's presence, respond to it.

__f__ Exodus 33:14   a. In God's presence is fullness of joy.

__a__ Psalm 16:11   b. The righteous will dwell in God's presence.

• **Zechariah 4:6**: "'Not by might nor by power, but by My Spirit,' says the LORD of hosts" (NKJV).

41

Discussion Questions

- Review last week's lesson, and give an overview of the W-E-L-L to which we turn for quenching our spiritual thirst:

_d_ Psalm 21:6   c. Come into God's presence with singing.

_g_ Psalm 68:8   d. In God's presence are gladness and blessing.

_c_ Psalm 100:2   e. In God's presence are times of refreshment.

_b_ Psalm 140:13   f. In God's presence is rest.

_e_ Acts 3:19   g. In God's presence the earth itself shakes.

6. David assures us, "The LORD is close to everyone who prays to him, to all who truly pray to him" (Ps. 145:18 NCV).

- What encouragement and promise was offered to Joshua in Joshua 1:9?
  <u>"Remember that I commanded you to be strong and brave. Don't be afraid, because the LORD your God will be with you everywhere you go" (Josh. 1:9 NCV).</u>

- What promise did Jesus make to his followers in Matthew 28:20?
  <u>"I will be with you always, even until the end of this age" (Matt. 28:20 NCV).</u>

- What dwells in us, according to John 14:17?
  <u>"The Spirit of truth ... you know Him, for He dwells with you and will be in you" (John 14:17 NKJV).</u>

"All believers have God in their hearts. But not all believers have given their whole heart to God."

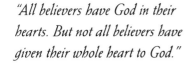

♦ What does Deuteronomy 30:14 say we should keep near to us?

<u>**"No, the word is very near you. It is in your mouth and in your heart so you may obey it"**</u>
<u>**(Deut. 30:14** NCV**).**</u>

Often we are called upon to wait awhile for the power we've prayed for. This doesn't mean twiddling our thumbs or busying ourselves elsewhere. We're still seeking. We're listening attentively for an answer. Waiting means watching. If you are waiting on a bus, you are watching for the bus. If you are waiting on God, you are watching for God, searching for God, hoping for God.

7. Knowing that God's presence is with us is a good thing. But it is infinitely better to seek God out. Go after him. Look for his hand. Search for him. Chase after him.

__f__ Ezra 7:10   a. Those who seek the Lord will praise Him.

__d__ Psalm 9:10   b. Those who seek Him will lack for nothing.

__a__ Psalm 22:26   c. Seek the Lord's face evermore.

__h__ Psalm 27:4   d. The LORD does not forsake those who seek Him.

Throughout the course of this study, we will be seeking out four ways in which our thirst can be satisfied. God's work. God's energy. His lordship and his love. You'll find them easy to remember. Just think of the word W-E-L-L.

*Receive Christ's **W**ork on the cross.*

*The **E**nergy of his Spirit.*

*His **L**ordship over your life.*

*His unending, unfailing **L**ove.*

Drink deeply and often. And out of you will flow rivers of living water.

- Would you say that your Christian walk is characterized by "energy"? If not, what other terms would you use to describe it?

- What kind of power is available to believers—*all* believers?

_b_ Psalm 34:10   e. Those who seek the Lord will rejoice.

_e_ Psalm 105:3   f. Your heart must be prepared to seek.

_c_ Psalm 105:4   g. Seek the Lord, seek righteousness, seek humility.

_i_ Isaiah 55:6   h. Seek the chance to see the beauty of the LORD.

_g_ Zephaniah 2:3   i. Seek the LORD while He may be found.

8. God is ready to be found by those who seek after him.

♦ What does David say that God is watching for in Psalm 14:2?
"The LORD looks down from heaven upon the children of men, to see if there are any who understand, who seek God" (Ps. 14:2 NKJV).

♦ What does God ask us to do, and what should our response be, according to Psalm 27:8?
God is watching for seekers, and he welcomes their pursuit. "When You said, 'Seek My face,' My heart said to You, 'Your face, LORD, I will seek'" (Ps. 27:8 NKJV).

"You can look for the LORD your God, and you will find him if you look for him with your whole being."

—Deuteronomy 4:29 NCV

♦ This is no casual game of hide-and-seek. How does Deuteronomy 4:29 say we should seek after God?

<u>God wants us searching for him, watching for him, following after him. "You will seek the LORD your God, and you will find Him if you seek Him with all your heart and with all your soul" (Deut. 4:29 NKJV). Seek and you shall find, so long as you throw yourself wholeheartedly into the search. God wants us all, heart, mind, and body.</u>

The Spirit fills as prayers flow. Desire to be filled with strength? Of course you do. Then pray, "Lord, I receive your energy. Empowered by your Holy Spirit, I can do all things through Christ who gives me strength."

9. It's not up to us. We can't depend on our own limited resources. Strength comes from God. Pray for his energy, for his power, for his Spirit.

"'Not by <u> might </u> (no amount of stamina, oomph or grit will help) nor by <u> power </u>, (don't rely on independence, authority, or willpower) but by <u> My </u> <u> Spirit </u>,' (spiritual strength is the power we need) says the Lord of hosts." (Zech. 4:6 NKJV)

• Max says, "Change your definition of prayer. Think of prayers as less an activity *for* God and more an awareness *of* God." How does this affect your days in a practical way? What changes?

• When is it hardest to wait for God's answer to our prayers?

45

• Field some of the questions that the conclusion of Lesson 3 asks:

What would life be like if you never learned about the energy available to us through the Holy Spirit? Would you live under the assumption that your spiritual walk was all up to you? Would you have to rely on your own strength, ingenuity, and willpower to please God? All the responsibility for your spiritual state would rest on your own shoulders. Fighting to stay spiritually afloat would burn you out. Your efforts toward righteous living would exhaust you. What kind of life would you lead?

10. When our heart thirsts for energy, we need only turn to the only Source of living water for the strength we need. "But You, O LORD, do not be far from Me; O My Strength, hasten to help Me!" (Ps. 22:19 NKJV).

Exodus 15:2: "The LORD is my __strength and song__"

2 Samuel 22:33: "God is my __strength and power__"

Psalm 73:26: "God is the __strength of my heart and my portion forever__"

Psalm 20:6: "He will answer __him from His holy heaven with the saving strength of His right hand__"

Conclusion

What would life be like if we never learned about the energy available to us through the Holy Spirit? Would you live under the assumption that your spiritual walk was all up to you? Would you have to rely on your own strength, ingenuity, and willpower to please God? All the responsibility for your spiritual state would rest on your own shoulders. Fighting to stay spiritually afloat would burn you out. Your efforts toward righteous living would exhaust you. What kind of life would you lead? A parched and prayerless one.

But what happens to the soul who seeks after God. What happens to the one who taps into God's vast resources? What happens to the person who believes in the work of the Spirit? Really believes. Is there a difference? Yes, indeed! Shoulders lift as the buckling weight of self-salvation drops away. Knees bend as they discover the power of the praying Spirit. And best of all, there abides a quiet confidence that comes from knowing it's not up to you.

Open It Up to Questions

Does anyone have any questions that came up over the week while reading either the book or the daily devotional readings?

47

Prayer of the Thirsty

Lift up this prayer once again to the Lord. You have learned what it means to receive his work. Now you are reaching out to him, asking to receive his energy. As you repeat this prayer again and again through the week ahead, remember where your strength comes from, and learn to rely on it.

Lord, I come thirsty. I come to drink, to receive. I receive Your work on the cross and in Your resurrection. My sins are pardoned and my death is defeated. I receive Your energy. Empowered by Your Holy Spirit, I can do all things through Christ who gives me strength. I receive Your lordship. I belong to You. Nothing comes to me that hasn't passed through You. And I receive Your love. Nothing can separate me from Your love.

This Week's Prayer Requests

Memory Verse

"Let us therefore come boldly
to the throne of grace, that we
may obtain mercy and find
grace to help in time of need."

—Hebrews 4:16 NKJV

Suggested Reading for this Week from *Come Thirsty* by Max Lucado:

- Chapter 6: "Hope for Tuckered Town"—Some of us try to live our Christian lives completely in our own power. God offers hope for us when the effort wears us down.

- Chapter 7: "Waiting for Power"—Before we move forward, sometimes God asks us to wait ... and pray.

- Chapter 8: "God's Body Glove"—The Holy Spirit works with us and through us, hand in glove.

- Chapter 9: "It's Not Up to You"—God paid too high a price for you to leave you unguarded. The Holy Spirit reminds us of our place in God's heart and comes to our aid in times of weakness.

W-E-L-L

Receive his Lordship over your life.

～∽ WEEK 4 ∽～

CHOOSING PEACE

"You cannot add any time to your life by worrying about it."

—Matthew 6:27 NCV

Introduction

What's to worry about? Plenty. We worry about big stuff and little stuff, things we did and things we're going to do, things we're responsible for and things we have no control over. Wouldn't you love to stop worrying? Could you use a strong shelter from life's harsh elements? God offers you just that. The possibility of a worry-free life. Not just less worry, but no worry.

You might be thinking, "Are you kidding?" Worry can be hard to shake. It comes so naturally to most of us. But Jesus wasn't kidding when he told us not to worry in this world. In fact, there are two words that summarize his opinion of worry: irrelevant and irreverent.

Opening Class

Option 1
Would you consider yourself a worrywart? Is it the big stuff or the little stuff that worries you?

Option 2
Are you a backseat driver? Do you like to maintain control of your life? Are you a self-reliant, independent person? How do these tendencies work against living a life of faith in God's ability to take care of you?

55

Option 3

There is something powerful when reading Scripture out loud together. Have people in the group look up this week's Scripture passages in various translations. Use them as a starting point for your lesson.

1. We worry every day about everyday things. Jesus knew this, and so he addressed our worries in the Gospels. What do each of these verses say we tend to worry over?

   ◆ Psalm 37:1: **Do not worry about evildoers (Ps. 37:1).**

   ◆ Psalm 37:7: **Do not worry when men plan wicked schemes (Ps. 37:7).**

   ◆ Matthew 6:25: **Do not worry about your life. (Matt. 6:25).**

   ◆ Matthew 6:28: **Do not worry about what you will wear (Matt. 6:28).**

   ◆ Matthew 6:31: **Do not worry about what you will eat or drink (Matt. 6:31).**

   ◆ Matthew 6:34: **Do not worry about tomorrow (Matt. 6:34).**

2. David advises, "Do not fret—it only causes harm" (Ps. 37:8 NKJV). What is the use of worrying, according to Jesus in Matthew 6:27? **"You cannot add any time to your life by worrying about it" (Matt. 6:27 NCV). Jesus dismisses worry as useless. Worry can't change things.**

Worry betrays a fragile faith. In essence we're saying we doubt God's ability to take care of us. We aren't so sure he knows what he's doing. We're not convinced that he has our best interests in mind. And so we're reluctant to give over control—to accept God's

lordship over our lives. It's subtle, even unintentional at times. But when we worry, we doubt God.

3. How could we possibly think that an all-powerful God might lose his grip? Or that an all-knowing God might make a mistake? Scripture is very clear. God *is* in control.

Psalm 115:3: "Our God is in heaven. He _does_ what he _pleases_." (NCV)

Isaiah 43:13: "I have _always_ been _God_ ....When I do something, no one can _change_ it." (NCV)

Isaiah 46:10: "When I _plan_ something, it _happens_. What I _want_ to do, I _will_ do." (NCV)

Lamentations 3:37: "Nobody can _speak_ and have it happen _unless_ the Lord _commands_ it." (NCV)

Acts 2:23: "This was God's _plan_ which he had made _long ago_; he knew all this would _happen_." (NCV)

Reading Scripture Out Loud

- **Psalm 37:8**: "Do not fret—it only causes harm" (NKJV).

- **Matthew 6:34**: "Do not worry about tomorrow" (NKJV).

- **Psalm 115:3**: "Our God is in heaven. He does what he pleases" (NCV).

- **Isaiah 46:10**: "When I plan something, it happens. What I want to do, I will do" (NCV).

- **Philippians 4:7**: "The peace of God, which surpasses all understanding, will guard your hearts and minds through Christ Jesus" (NKJV).

- Colossians 3:15: "Let the peace of God rule in your hearts, to which also you were called in one body; and be thankful" (NKJV).

- 1 Peter 5:7: "Casting all your care upon Him, for He cares for you" (NKJV).

- Ephesians 1:11: "In Christ we were chosen to be God's people, because from the very beginning God had decided this in keeping with his plan. And he is the One who makes everything agree with what he decides and wants" (NCV).

Acts 17:25: "This God is the One who gives life, breath, and everything else to people. He does not need any __help__ from them; he has __everything__ he __needs__." (NCV)

Ephesians 1:11: "In Christ we were chosen to be God's people, because from the very beginning God had __decided__ this in keeping with his __plan__. And he is the One who makes everything __agree__ with what he __decides__ and __wants__." (NCV)

According to the Bible, God is worthy of all the glory he receives. He does as he pleases. Who are we to question it? But we often have trouble accepting this because it goes against our own agendas. We pursue the wrong priority. We want good health, good income, a good night's rest, and a good retirement. Our priority is *we*. God's priority, however, is God.

4. God always knows what is best. We don't always like it, but what else can we say?

   ♦ What does Isaiah 45:7 say God is able to do? **"I made the light and the darkness. I bring peace, and I cause troubles. I, the LORD, do all these things" (Is. 45:7 NCV).**

   ♦ What does Solomon urge us to remember in Ecclesiastes 7:14?

"When life is good, enjoy it. But when life is hard, remember: God gives good times and hard times, and no one knows what tomorrow will bring" (Eccl. 7:14 NCV).

🔥 What is God able to command according to Lamentations 3:38?
"Both bad and good things come by the command of the Most High God" (Lam. 3:38 NCV).

🔥 And according to Isaiah 48:10, 11, why does God do these things?
"I have made you pure, but not by fire, as silver is made pure. I have purified you by giving you troubles. I do this for myself, for my own sake. I will not let people speak evil against me, and I will not let some god take my glory" (Is. 48:10, 11 NCV).

Worry comes from the Greek word that means "to divide the mind." Anxiety splits us right down the middle, creating a double-minded thinker. Perception is divided, distorting our vision. Strength is divided, wasting our energy.

How can we stop doing so? Paul offers a two-pronged answer: "Do not worry about anything, but pray and ask God for everything you need, always giving thanks" (Phil. 4:6 NCV). Our part in staving off worry includes prayer and gratitude.

Discussion Questions

• *Come Thirsty* urges you to return to the W.E.L.L. Take a few minutes to run through the outline of the lesson plans with your group.

Throughout the course of this study, we will be seeking out four ways in which our thirst can be satisfied. God's work. God's energy. His lordship and his love. You'll find them easy to remember. Just think of the word W-E-L-L.

Receive Christ's Work on the cross.

The Energy of his Spirit.

His Lordship over your life.

His unending, unfailing Love.
    Drink deeply and often. And out of you will flow rivers of living water.

- What does it mean to say that worry is irrelevant? What does it mean to say that worry is irreverent?

- Psalm 37:8 says "Do not fret—it only causes harm." What harm does worry cause?

- When it comes to the character of God, you've heard of the three O's— omnipresent, omniscient, omnipotent. When we say God is omnipotent— all-powerful—do we really believe that he can do anything? When we say God is omniscient—all-seeing —do we really believe that he is sovereign? How do these facts translate into our everyday lives? What is the practical result of these truths?

5. The first strategy to purge the worry out of your life is prayer. Paul says not to worry, but to pray.

♦ What does Luke 18:1 say we should always do, and never do?
Jesus said that his followers should "always pray and never lose hope" (Luke 18:1 NCV).

♦ Who should pray, according to James 5:13?
"Anyone who is having troubles should pray," according to James 5:13.

♦ How does Paul say we should pray in Colossians 4:2?
And Paul says that we should "continue praying" (Col. 4:2 NCV). Don't stop praying.

6. The second thing Paul urges is thanksgiving. Worry has a hard time taking hold of a heart that is thanking God for his faithfulness in the past. Why should we be thankful, according to Psalm 107:8?

"Oh, that men would give thanks to the LORD for His goodness, and for His wonderful works to the children of men!" (Ps. 107:8 NKJV). We give thanks for God's goodness. Though we do not always understand them, all his works are wonderful.

Our part is prayer and thanksgiving. What's God's part? Peace. Believing prayer ushers in God's peace. Not a random, nebulous, earthly peace, but his peace. God does not battle anxiety. God enjoys perfect peace because God enjoys perfect power. And he offers his peace to you.

7. Peace

   __b__ Numbers 6:26   a. May the Lord of peace give you peace always.

   __e__ Luke 1:79   b. May the LORD watch over you and give you peace.

   __c__ John 14:27   c. Peace I leave with you; My peace I give to you.

   __a__ Romans 3:17   d. Only those who belong to God will find peace.

   __d__ 2 Thessalonians 3:16   e. God will guide our feet into the way of peace.

Peace is precious because there is no substitute. Lust may masquerade as love, and happiness might try to stand in for joy, but there is no mimic for peace.

- Lordship can be a touchy subject for some people. Let's make sure we're all on the same page. What is meant by lordship? How can God's lordship be a source of strength and sustenance for our thirsting hearts?

- How do prayer and thanksgiving counteract the plague of worry?

- What does it mean to say, "peace rules in our hearts"? How is this peace able to then guard our hearts?

"Jesus used this story to teach his followers that they should always pray and never lose hope."

—Luke 18:1 NCV

61

Open It Up to Questions

Does anyone have any questions that came up over the week while reading either the book or the daily devotional readings?

"Don't look forward in fear, look backward in appreciation. God's proof is God's past. Forgetfulness sires fearfulness, but a good memory makes for a good heart."

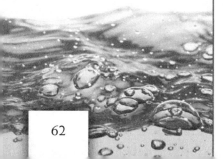

8. What is the peace of God able to do, according to Philippians 4:7?

"The peace of God, which surpasses all understanding, will guard your hearts and minds through Christ Jesus" (Phil. 4:7 NKJV**). God's peace is an amazing thing. It does something that is beyond belief, that defies comprehension. The peace of God is able to guard your mind. What's more, it is able to guard your heart. When the peace of God is in place, you cannot be attacked by life's worries and fears.**

9. If we want a heart filled with peace rather than worry, what must we let peace do, according to Colossians 3:15?

"Let the peace of God rule in your hearts, to which also you were called in one body; and be thankful" (Col. 3:15 NKJV**). Let peace rule. Let it. Don't allow worries to drown out its quiet voice. Tune your ears to it. Hang on to its promise. And let it reign in your life.**

Letting go of worries means letting God know that you trust him. We need to let peace rule in our hearts. Sure, worries and fears might try to usurp the throne, but the peace that rules is also the peace that guards.

10. What does 1 Peter 5:7 say that we should do with all our worries and cares?

"Casting all your care upon Him, for He cares for you" (1 Pet. 5:7 NKJV). Give them up. Pitch them aside. Cast them on to the One who is strong enough to bear them. But whatever you do, don't cling to them.

"Cast." Not place, lay, or occasionally offer. Strong verb there. Peter enlists the same verb gospel writers used to describe the way Jesus treated demons. "He cast them out." An authoritative hand on the collar, another on the belt, and a "Don't come back." Do the same with your fears. Get serious with them. Immediately cast them upon God.

Conclusion

God can lead you into a worry-free world. Amazing, but true. So be quick to pray. Focus less on the problems ahead and more on the victories behind. Trust his sovereignty. Let him be the Lord. You do your part and God will do his. He will guard your heart with his peace...a peace that passes understanding.

Prayer of the Thirsty

We come once again to the prayer of the thirsty.

Lord, I come thirsty. I come to drink, to receive. I receive Your work on the cross and in Your resurrection. My sins are pardoned and my death is defeated. I receive Your energy. Empowered by Your Holy Spirit, I can do all things through Christ who gives me strength. I receive Your lordship. I belong to You. Nothing comes to me that hasn't passed through You. And I receive Your love. Nothing can separate me from Your love.

THIS WEEK'S PRAYER REQUESTS

Memory Verse

*"Be anxious for nothing, but
in everything by prayer and
supplication, with thanksgiving,
let your requests be made known
to God; and the peace of God,
which surpasses all understanding,
will guard your hearts and
minds through Christ Jesus."*

—Philippians 4:6, 7 NKJV

Suggested Reading for this Week from *Come Thirsty* by Max Lucado:

- Chapter 10: "In God We (Nearly) Trust"—We know that God knows what's best. We know that we don't. We also know that God cares, so we can trust him.

- Chapter 11: "Worry? You Don't Have To"—Worry changes nothing, and only shows that we aren't trusting God to do as he promised.

- Chapter 12: "Angels Watching Over You"—When you accept God's lordship in your life, you can be assured that many mighty angels will guard you in all your ways.

- Chapter 13: "With God as Your Guardian"—God guards those who turn to him.

W-E-L-L

Receive his unending, unfailing Love.

WEEK 5

ABIDING IN GOD'S LOVE

"As the Father loved Me,
I also have loved you;
abide in My love."

—John 15:9 NKJV

Introduction

Are you familiar with 1 Corinthians 13? It is often referred to as the "Love Chapter," as it highlights the many facets of pure, godly love. "Love is patient. Love is kind. Love is not boastful or rude." Familiar and reassuring words. Often, we are invited to insert our own name into the wording of the chapter, personalizing it. "Jane is not easily provoked. Bill thinks no evil. Amanda bears all things." But have you ever considered that all these admirable qualities also apply to God in his love for us? When we say that God loves us, we can rest assured that God's love for us is patient. His love for us is kind. In his great love for us, he bears with us and rejoices when we choose good things. Love never fails, and neither does God.

Opening Class

Option 1

We speak casually of the things we love, meaning instead that these are our favorite things. "I love Starbucks® coffee" or "I love football" don't really constitute true love. For fun, have the class share some of their favorite things, and some of the things they love. Then ask them to consider the fact that they are one of God's favorite things, and he has bestowed his great love on them!

71

Option 2

Have you ever loved someone and been loved in return? How did that change your outlook on life? How did that sureness of another's love give you strength?

Option 3

There is something powerful when reading Scripture out loud together. Have people in the group look up this week's Scripture passages in various translations. Use them as a starting point for your lesson.

1. When you want to learn about love, you must start at the source. What are the beloved disciple's familiar words in 1 John 4:7, 8?

" __Beloved__ , let us __love__ one another, for __love__ is of God; and everyone who __loves__ is born of God and knows God. He who does not __love__ does not know God, for __God is love.__" (1 John 4:7, 8 NKJV)

2. What does God's love for us look like?
   - How did God demonstrate his love for us, according to Romans 5:8?
   __"God demonstrates His own love toward us, in that while we were still sinners, Christ died for us"__ (Rom. 5:8 NKJV).

   - When we are saved, what does God do, according to Romans 5:5?
   __God loved us enough to die for us. "The love of God has been poured out in our hearts by the Holy Spirit who was given to us"__ (Rom. 5:5 NKJV).

♦ Because of God's great love for us, what does he call us, according to 1 John 3:1?
God's love is poured over us. We are drenched in it. "Behold what manner of love the Father has bestowed on us, that we should be called children of God" (1 John 3:1 NKJV). God loves us so much that he's adopted us into his family. He calls us his own children.

God pours out his love on his children. It's more than bucketfuls. It's more than pond-fuls. It's more than lake-fuls. It's more than ocean-fuls. We're drenched in it. Saturated by it. Soaked to the skin. But we cannot be soaked to the very soul if we do not drink it in.

3. How does Jeremiah 31:3 characterize God's love for us?
"I have loved you with an everlasting love; therefore with lovingkindness I have drawn you" (Jer. 31:3 NKJV). The Message paraphrases this verse: "I've never quit loving you and never will. Expect love, love, and more love!"

We already know that God is changeless. "I am the LORD, I do not change" (Mal. 3:6 NKJV). It is not strange to discover that God's love is also changeless. "I have loved you with an everlasting love" (Jer. 31:3 NKJV). Everlasting. Eternal. Never-ending. Always. Ceaseless. Unchangeable. Forever. Ever after.

Reading Scripture Out Loud

- **Romans 5:8**: "God demonstrates His own love toward us, in that while we were still sinners, Christ died for us" (NKJV).

- **1 John 3:1**: "Behold what manner of love the Father has bestowed on us, that we should be called children of God!" (NKJV).

"God has poured out his love to fill our hearts. He gave us his love through the Holy Spirit, whom God has given to us."

—Romans 5:5 NCV

- **1 John 4:7, 8**: "Beloved, let us love one another, for love is of God; and everyone who loves is born of God and knows God. He who does not love does not know God, for God is love" (NKJV).

- **Jeremiah 31:3**: "I have loved you with an everlasting love; therefore with lovingkindness I have drawn you" (NKJV).

- **1 John 4:19**: "We love Him because He first loved us" (NKJV).

"[God] loves you because he is he. He loves you because he decides to. Self-generated, uncaused, and spontaneous; his constant-level love depends on his choice to give it."

4. In what way does God show his love in Zephaniah 3:17?
   <u>"The LORD your God in your midst, the Mighty One, will save; He will rejoice over you with gladness, He will quiet you with His love, He will rejoice over you with singing" (Zeph. 3:17 NKJV).</u>

5. When you are out on the ocean, you are completely surrounded by water. When you are up in an airplane, there is nothing but clouds and sky. Astronauts who leave our atmosphere are surrounded by star-flecked space. What surrounds believers, according to Ephesians 3:17–19?
   <u>Paul prays that, "You, being rooted and grounded in love, may be able to comprehend with all the saints what is the width and length and depth and height—to know the love of Christ which passes knowledge" (Eph. 3:17–19 NKJV). God surrounds us with his love.</u>

Over and around us, as far as the eye can see and beyond. God's love for us is so great, we cannot comprehend its immensity. Paul prays that believers might root themselves into it, drawing strength from it. He wants for us to catch a glimpse of something too big to grasp. It is beyond measure. It is unsearchable in its magnitude. For the love of God is as big as God. After all, God *is* love.

6. The pages of Scripture are filled with love. The love of God. The love of Jesus. The love of believers. Here is just a sampling. Match up the truth with the Bible passage in which it is located.

_e_ Psalm 36:7   a. The God of love will be with you.

_h_ John 13:34   b. God makes His home with those He loves.

_b_ John 14:23   c. Speak the truth in love.

_i_ 2 Corinthians 5:14   d. There is comfort in love.

_a_ 2 Corinthians 13:11   e. God's lovingkindness is precious to His children.

_m_ Ephesians 2:4   f. Keep yourselves in the love of God.

_g_ Ephesians 3:19   g. The love of Christ passes all knowledge.

_c_ Ephesians 4:15   h. Love one another as I have loved you.

• **Romans 8:38, 39**: "Yes, I am sure that neither death, nor life, nor angels, nor ruling spirits, nothing now, nothing in the future, no powers, nothing above us, nothing below us, nor anything else in the whole world will ever be able to separate us from the love of God that is in Christ Jesus our Lord" (NCV).

75

Discussion Questions

- Please take a few moments to review the outline of the *Come Thirsty* lessons again with your people before moving forward with this week's lesson.

Throughout the course of this study, we will be seeking out four ways in which our thirst can be satisfied. God's work. God's energy. His lordship and his love. You'll find them easy to remember. Just think of the word W-E-L-L.

"He knows you better than you know you and he has reached his verdict. He loves you still. No discovery will disillusion him, no rebellion will dissuade him. He loves you with an everlasting love."

_k_ Ephesians 5:2	i. The love of Christ compels us.
_d_ Philippians 2:1	j. God directs our hearts into His love.
_l_ Colossians 2:2	k. Walk in love.
_j_ 2 Thessalonians 3:5	l. Believers are knit together in love.
_f_ Jude 1:21	m. God has loved us with a great love.

7. What does Jesus ask us to do in John 15:9, 10?

"As the __Father loved__ Me, I also have __loved__ you; abide in My love. If you keep My commandments, you will abide in My love, just as I have kept My Father's commandments and abide in His love" (John 15:9, 10 NKJV).

To abide in Christ's love is to make his love our home. Settle in. Set up housekeeping. Make ourselves comfortable. When you abide somewhere, you live there. You grow familiar with the surroundings. Jesus abided in God's love. We are invited to abide in Christ's. By doing so, "in this world we are like him" (1 John 4:17 NCV).

8. What is Jesus' idea of abiding, according to John 15:4, 5?

"Remain in me, and I will remain in you. A branch cannot produce fruit alone but must remain in the vine. In the same way, you cannot produce fruit alone but must remain in me. I am the vine, and you are the branches. If any remain in me and I remain in them, they produce much fruit. But without me they can do nothing" (John 15:4, 5 NCV).

According to Jesus, the branch models his definition of "abiding." The branch must be connected to the vine in order to live, grow, and bear fruit. Without the vine, a branch is useless. It can do nothing. We need to hang on to Christ as a branch clutches the vine. If we don't, we go thirsty.

9. With a God who draws us with lovingkindness and promises everlasting love, how can we resist? What is the response of believers to God's outpouring, according to 1 John 4:19? **"We love Him because He first loved us"** (1 John 4:19 NKJV).

We cannot earn God's love. We cannot barter for it. We cannot plead with God to love us. It would be useless to try, because he already does. He loved us first. All we can do is respond to God's love, abide in his love, love in return.

10. What question does Paul raise in Romans 8:35? And what resounding promise is the answer, found in verses 38 and 39?

*Receive Christ's **W**ork on the cross.*

*The **E**nergy of his Spirit.*

*His **L**ordship over your life.*

*His unending, unfailing **L**ove. Drink deeply and often. And out of you will flow rivers of living water.*

- God loves those he has created, but there is a difference between being loved and accepting that love. What changes in the human heart when it understands the love of God and returns it?

"You don't influence God's love. You can't impact the tree-ness of a tree, the sky-ness of the sky, or the rock-ness of a rock. Nor can you affect the love of God."

- As humans, we often bestow our love on others *because* of who they are or what they have done. We might harbor ulterior motives. Often, we have conditions: "I will love you if you will …" or "I will love you as long as you …" or "I will love you until …" What do we look for in those we choose to love?

- God loves because he is love, and that love is unconditional. Nothing we do can change his love. What hope does this give to sinners—to all of us?

> Paul's question: "Can anything separate us from the love Christ has for us? Can troubles or problems or sufferings or hunger or nakedness or danger or violent death?" (Rom. 8:35 NCV). The answer: "Yes, I am sure that neither death, nor life, nor angels, nor ruling spirits, nothing now, nothing in the future, no powers, nothing above us, nothing below us, nor anything else in the whole world will ever be able to separate us from the love of God that is in Christ Jesus our Lord" (Rom. 8:38, 39 NCV).

Nothing can separate us from the love of God. Paul is convinced of this! "I am convinced that nothing can ever separate us from his love." He uses the perfect tense, implying: "I have become and I remain convinced." This is no passing idea or fluffy thought, but rather a deeply rooted conviction. Paul is absolutely sure. You can be, too!

Conclusion

Nothing can shake your Heavenly Father's love for you. God knows your entire story, from first word to final breath, and with clear assessment declares, "You are mine." Step to the well of his love and drink up. Occasional drinks won't bedew the evaporated heart. Ceaseless swallows will. Take your fill. The supply is boundless, everlasting.

Prayer of the Thirsty

We return to this prayer of the thirsty soul. It is the prayer of a heart ready to receive God's love. Unconditional, unreserved, immeasurable love. Take the time each day to pray this prayer aloud. Let it recall to your heart and mind just how precious you are to the Father.

Lord, I come thirsty. I come to drink, to receive. I receive Your work on the cross and in Your resurrection. My sins are pardoned and my death is defeated. I receive Your energy. Empowered by Your Holy Spirit, I can do all things through Christ who gives me strength. I receive Your lordship. I belong to You. Nothing comes to me that hasn't passed through You. And I receive Your love. Nothing can separate me from Your love.

- We are invited to abide in Christ's love. What is this compared to? (*To abide in Christ's love is to make his love our home. Settle in. Set up housekeeping. Make ourselves comfortable. When you abide somewhere, you live there. You grow familiar with the surroundings. Also, according to Jesus, the branch models his definition of "abiding." The branch must be connected to the vine in order to live, grow, and bear fruit.*)

- Can we exert influence over God? Can we make him do anything? Can we affect him, change him? Then why do we try to earn our place in his heart?

- Why does knowing that we are loved change us? Why does knowing that we are loved strengthen us?

79

THIS WEEK'S PRAYER REQUESTS

Memory Verse

*"Yes, I am sure that neither death,
nor life, nor angels, nor ruling
spirits, nothing now, nothing in
the future, no powers, nothing
above us, nothing below us, nor
anything else in the whole world
will ever be able to separate us
from the love of God that is
in Christ Jesus our Lord."*

—Romans 8:38, 39 NCV

Prayer of the Thirsty

*Lord, I come thirsty. I come to
drink, to receive. I receive Your
work on the cross and in your
resurrection. My sins are
pardoned and my death is
defeated. I receive Your energy.
Empowered by Your Holy
Spirit, I can do all things
through Christ who gives
me strength. I receive Your
lordship. I belong to You.
Nothing comes to me that
hasn't passed through You.
And I receive Your love.
Nothing can separate me from
Your love.*

Open It Up
to Questions

Does anyone have any
questions that came up
over the week while
reading either the book
or the daily devotional
readings?

Suggested Reading for this Week from *Come Thirsty* by Max Lucado:

- Chapter 14: "Going Deep"—Plunge into the depths of the limitless love of God.
- Chapter 15: "Have You Heard the Clanging Door?"—Some fear they've gone too far, done too much, wandered too long to be worthy of God's love. But the God who knows everything about you loves you still.
- Chapter 16: "Fearlessly Facing Eternity"—God knows our imperfections, yet has chosen us. We need never fear God's judgment. Trust His love.
- Chapter 17: "If God Wrote You a Letter"—If God sent you a personal letter, it might read something like this.

NOTES

W-E-L-L

Receive Christ's Work on the cross.

Receive the Energy of his Spirit.

Receive his Lordship over your life.

Receive his unending, unfailing Love.

WEEK 6

IF GOD WROTE YOU A LETTER

"The LORD will guide you continually, and satisfy your soul in drought, and strengthen your bones; you shall be like a watered garden, and like a spring of water, whose waters do not fail."

—Isaiah 58:11 NKJV

Introduction

The final chapter of Max's *Come Thirsty* asks you to pause and consider, what if God wrote you a letter? In a way, he did. The Scriptures stand as a lengthy piece of correspondence from the Father's heart to his people. Max takes the time to condense God's message in a way that speaks to our thirsting hearts. Let's take a more careful look at the promises this letter holds.

Opening Class

Option 1

Many people keep a prayer journal. In a sense, they are writing out their prayers as a letter to God. Poll your group. Has anyone tried this? What value has it shown in their spiritual walk? Would anyone else in the group like to begin such a journal?

87

Option 2

Many of the books in our Bible are epistles—letters penned by the leaders of the early Christian church. Others are prophecies, written records of the words of God, as received by the prophets. Either way, Scripture says that they were written by inspiration of God. They are God's words—God's Word—for us. Have you ever considered the fact that your Bible was written so that God could reveal himself to you? Does that change how you look at your Bible?

We'll take the letter in small sections. Take your time. Meditate over each of these verses. Consider what God is telling you about himself. What does he want you to know? What is he promising you? Then give yourself time to respond. What would happen if this was a dialogue? What would be your reply? Consider what you would like to tell God in return.

If God Wrote You a Letter

Are you thirsty? Come and drink. I am One who comforts you. I bought you. I complete you. I delight in you and claim you as my own, rejoicing over you as a bridegroom rejoices over his bride. I will never fail nor forsake you.

  e   Isaiah 55:1   a. You were bought at a price.

  c   Isaiah 51:12   b. The LORD delights in you and rejoices over you.

  a   1 Corinthians 6:20   c. I am He who comforts you.

  f   Colossians 2:10   d. He will never leave you nor forsake you.

  b   Isaiah 62:4, 5   e. Everyone who thirsts, come to the waters.

88

__d__ Hebrews 13:5   f. You are complete in
                           Him.

Accept My Work

I know your manifold transgressions and your mighty sins, yet my grace is sufficient for you. I have cast all your sins behind my back, trampled them under my feet, and thrown them into the depths of the ocean! Your sins have been washed away, swept away like the morning mists, scattered like the clouds. O return to me, for I have paid the price to set you free.

__d__ Amos 5:12   a. God has cast all
                          your sins behind
                          His back.

__f__ 2 Corinthians 12:9   b. You have been
                              washed, sanctified,
                              justified.

__a__ Isaiah 38:17   c. Our transgressions
                          have been blotted
                          out.

__e__ Micah 7:19   d. He knows all about
                          your transgressions.

__b__ 1 Corinthians 6:11   e. All our sins have
                              been cast into the
                              sea.

Option 3

There is something powerful when reading Scripture out loud together. Have people in the group look up this week's Scripture passages in various translations. Use them as a starting point for your lesson.

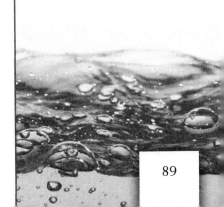

89

Reading Scripture Out Loud

- **Isaiah 55:1**: "Ho! Everyone who thirsts, come to the waters" (NKJV).

- **Colossians 2:10**: "You are complete in Him, who is the head of all principality and power." (NKJV).

- **Isaiah 38:17**: "You have lovingly delivered my soul from the pit of corruption, for You have cast all my sins behind Your back" (NKJV).

- **2 Corinthians 4:1**: "As we have received mercy, we do not lose heart" (NKJV).

_c_ Isaiah 44:22

f. God's grace is sufficient.

Your death is swallowed up in victory. I disarmed the evil rulers and authorities and broke the power of the devil, who had the power of death. Blessed are those who die in the Lord. Your citizenship is in heaven. Come, inherit the kingdom prepared for you where I will remove all of your sorrows, and there will be no more death or sorrow or crying or pain.

_e_ 1 Corinthians 15:54

a. Blessed are those who die in the Lord.

_b_ Colossians 2:15

b. Principalities and powers have been disarmed.

_f_ Hebrews 2:14

c. We shall inherit a kingdom prepared for us.

_a_ Revelation 14:13

d. Every tear shall be wiped away.

_g_ Philippians 3:20

e. Death is swallowed up in victory.

_d_ Matthew 25:34

f. He has destroyed the devil's power over death.

_c_ Revelation 21:4   g. Our citizenship is in heaven.

Rely on My Energy

You are worried and troubled about many things; trust me with all your heart.

I know how to rescue godly people from their trials. My Spirit helps you in your distress. Let me strengthen you with my glorious power. I did not spare my Son but gave him up for you. Won't I give you everything else? March on, dear soul, with courage! Never give up. I will help you. I will uphold you.

_e_ Luke 10:41   a. We are strengthened by God's glorious power.

_i_ Proverbs 3:5   b. We do not lose heart.

_d_ 2 Peter 2:9   c. God gives us freely of all the things we need.

_g_ Romans 8:26   d. The LORD knows how to deliver the godly.

_a_ Colossians 1:11   e. You are worried and troubled about many things.

_c_ Romans 8:32   f. March on in strength.

- **Romans 8:32**: "He who did not spare His own Son, but delivered Him up for us all, how shall He not with Him also freely give us all things?" (NKJV).

- **Isaiah 26:3**: "You will keep him in perfect peace, whose mind is stayed on You, because he trusts in You" (NKJV).

- **Psalm 139:10**: "Even there Your hand shall lead me, and Your right hand shall hold me" (NKJV).

- **Philippians 4:6**: "Be anxious for nothing, but in everything by prayer and supplication, with thanksgiving, let your requests be made known to God" (NKJV).

- **Romans 8:31**: "What then shall we say to these things? If God is for us, who can be against us?" (NKJV).

__f__ Judges 5:21   g. The Spirit helps us in our weaknesses.

__b__ 2 Corinthians 4:1   h. God will help you. He will uphold you.

__h__ Isaiah 41:10   i. Trust in the LORD with all your heart.

Trust My Lordship

Trust in me always. I am the eternal Rock, your Shepherd, the Guardian of your soul. When you go through deep waters and great trouble, I will be with you. When you go through rivers of difficulty, you will not drown! When you walk through the fire of oppression, you will not be burned up; the flames will not consume you.

__b__ Isaiah 26:3, 4   a. He is the Shepherd and Overseer of our souls.

__a__ 1 Peter 2:25   b. God will keep us in perfect peace.

__c__ Isaiah 43:2   c. He will be with you through everything.

So don't worry. I never tire or sleep. I stand beside you. The angel of the LORD encamps around you. I hide you in the shelter of My presence. I will go ahead of you directing your steps and delighting in every detail of your life. If you stumble, you will not fall, for I hold you by the hand. I will guide you along the best pathway for your life. Wars will break out near and far, but don't panic. I have overcome the world. Don't worry about anything; instead, pray about everything. I surround you with a shield of love.

__i__ Matthew 6:34

a. Be strong, don't be afraid, God goes with you.

__c__ Psalm 121:3

b. He holds our hand and leads us.

__f__ Psalm 34:7

c. He who keeps you will not slumber.

__j__ Psalm 31:20

d. He has overcome the world.

__a__ Deuteronomy 31:6

e. Don't fear when you hear rumors of war.

__h__ Psalm 37:23, 24

f. The angel of the LORD encamps around God's people.

__b__ Psalm 139:10

g. The LORD will bless the righteous.

- **Psalm 139:17, 18**: "How precious also are Your thoughts to me, O God! How great is the sum of them! If I should count them, they would be more in number than the sand; When I awake, I am still with You" (NKJV). "casting all your care upon Him, for He cares for you (1 Pet. 5:7 NKJV).

- **Revelation 22:17**: "And the Spirit and the bride say, 'Come!' And let him who hears say, 'Come!' And let him who thirsts come. Whoever desires, let him take the water of life freely" (NKJV).

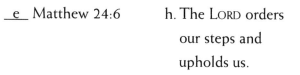

Discussion Questions

- Take a few minutes to review the lessons of the last several weeks. The outline is simple, but there is a rich complexity to be found within.

_e_ Matthew 24:6

_d_ John 16:33

_k_ Philippians 4:6

_g_ Psalm 5:12

h. The LORD orders our steps and upholds us.

i. Do not worry about tomorrow.

j. God will hide us and keep us secretly.

k. Be anxious for nothing, but pray.

I will make you fruitful in the land of suffering, trading beauty for ashes, joy for mourning, praise for despair. I live with the low-spirited and spirit-crushed. I put a new spirit in you and get you on your feet again. Weeping may go on all night, but joy comes with the morning. If I am for you, who can ever be against you?

_c_ Genesis 41:52

_e_ Isaiah 61:1–3

_a_ Isaiah 57:15

_b_ Psalm 30:5

_d_ Romans 8:31

a. God dwells with those who are humble.

b. Joy comes in the morning.

c. God has caused me to be fruitful.

d. If God is for us, who can be against us?

e. God will trade beauty for your ashes.

Receive My Love

I throw my arms around you, lavish attention on you and guard you like the apple of my eye. I rejoice over you with great gladness. My thoughts of you cannot be counted; they outnumber the grains of sand! Nothing can ever separate you from my love. Death can't, and life can't. The angels can't, and the demons can't. Your fears for today, your worries about tomorrow, and even the powers of hell can't keep my love away.

_d_ Deuteronomy 32:10	a. Nothing can separate us from Christ's love.
_b_ Zephaniah 3:17	b. God will save you, rejoice over you, quiet you.
_c_ Psalm 139:17, 18	c. God's thoughts of you are precious.
_a_ Romans 8:35	d. We are kept as the apple of God's eye.

Throughout the course of this study, we will be seeking out four ways in which our thirst can be satisfied. God's work. God's energy. His lordship and his love. You'll find them easy to remember. Just think of the word W-E-L-L.

*Receive Christ's **W**ork on the cross.*

*The **E**nergy of his Spirit.*

*His **L**ordship over your life.*

*His unending, unfailing **L**ove.*
Drink deeply and often. And out of you will flow rivers of living water.

- Scripture is filled with promises. This week's "Letter from God" holds many of these precious promises. What makes these promises more trustworthy than the promises of people?

- If the promises of God are so certain, do you believe them? If you believe them, do you act upon them?

- Now that you know about the "W E L L" and have spent the last few weeks drinking from it, are you done? Can you move on now? Why must we return to these things continually?

You sometimes say, "The Lord has deserted us; the Lord has forgotten us." But can a mother forget her nursing child? Can she feel no love for a child she has borne? But even if that were possible, I would not forget you! I paid for you with the precious lifeblood of Christ, my sinless, spotless Lamb. No one will snatch you away from me. See, I have written your name on my hand. I call you my friend. Why, the very hairs on your head are all numbered. So, don't be afraid; you are valuable to me.

_e_ Isaiah 49:14, 15   a. No one can snatch us from His hand.

_b_ 1 Peter 1:19   b. You're bought with Christ's precious blood.

_a_ John 10:28   c. Even your hairs are numbered.

_f_ Isaiah 49:16   d. Christ has called you His friends.

_d_ John 15:15   e. God cannot forget you.

_c_ Matthew 10:29–31   f. Your name is inscribed on His hands.

Give me your burdens, I will take care of you. I know how weak you are; that you are made of dust. Give all your worries and cares to me, for I care about what happens to you. Remember, I am at hand. Come to me when you are weary and carry heavy burdens, and I will give you rest. I delight in you; and can be trusted to keep my promise. Come and drink the water of life.

_d_	Psalm 55:22	a. The Lord is at hand.
_g_	Psalm 103:13, 14	b. If you thirst, come and drink freely.
_e_	1 Peter 5:7	c. The LORD takes pleasure in His people.
_a_	Philippians 4:5	d. Cast your burden on the LORD; He will sustain you.
_h_	Matthew 11:28	e. Cast your cares upon Him, He cares for you.
_c_	Psalm 149:4	f. He who makes us promises is faithful.
_f_	Hebrews 10:23	g. God remembers that we are made of dust.
_b_	Revelation 22:17	h. Come to Me and I will give you rest.

Your Maker, Your Father,
God

- Work. Energy. Lordship. Love. Which of these four has come into clearer focus over the last five weeks? What lessons have you learned?

Open It Up to Questions

Does anyone have any questions that came up over the week while reading either the book or the daily devotional readings?

Conclusion

Promises. Each and every one of those verses you just looked up holds precious and powerful promises. Do you believe them? Then soak in them. Drink them up. And don't stop there. Drink, and keep drinking. Return to them, and to the One who promised them. He holds everything you will ever need.

Prayer of the Thirsty

One more time, pray the prayer of the thirsty.
But don't let it be the last time. You cannot saturate
a dehydrated heart by one quick gulp. Return over
and over to soak. Let this prayer remind you of the
wellspring of life—God's work, his energy, his lordship,
and his love. Yours for the asking.

*Lord, I come thirsty. I come to drink, to receive. I receive
Your work on the cross and in Your resurrection. My
sins are pardoned and my death is defeated. I receive Your
energy. Empowered by Your Holy Spirit, I can do all
things through Christ who gives me strength. I receive
Your lordship. I belong to You. Nothing comes to me
that hasn't passed through You. And I receive Your love.
Nothing can separate me from Your love.*

This Week's Prayer Requests

Memory Verse

"The LORD will guide you continually, and satisfy your soul in drought, and strengthen your bones; you shall be like a watered garden, and like a spring of water, whose waters do not fail."

—Isaiah 58:11 NKJV

NOTES

NOTES

NOTES

ALSO AVAILABLE FOR YOUR CHURCH,

The *Come Thirsty* Experience

Many leaders are already asking the question, "What's the next church program?" Max Lucado's *Come Thirsty* Experience offers every church of every size a 6-week program with 3 levels of participation available. Some features of this unique campaign for your church will include:

- 6-week worship plan: sermon outlines and illustrations, music and Scripture reading suggestions
- Adult study and leaders' materials for small groups
- Youth study and leaders' materials for small groups
- Children's resources featuring Hermie™: object lessons and craft/activity suggestions, take-home papers, and coloring pages. All fully reproducible!
- DVD and VHS resource: 7 minute teaching sessions lead by Max Lucado
- *Come & Drink* daily devotionals for the 6 weeks
- A 6-week reading plan for *Come Thirsty*
- An outreach package that includes mini-invites, brochures, and much more!
- Nelson's Exclusive CD-ROM: customize and create your own posters/bulletin inserts/flyers
- 30-second video promo by Max Lucado introducing the series
- PowerPoint™ template
- And much more!

NELSON REFERENCE & ELECTRONIC
A Division of Thomas Nelson Publishers
Since 1798

www.thomasnelson.com

Available at your favorite
Christian Bookstore and
www.comethirsty.com

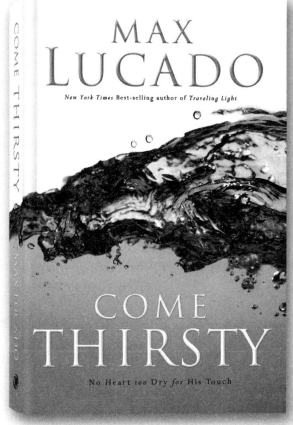